FEB 14 1997
MAR 11 1997

MAY 28 1997

W9-BTO-294

Laubach Way to Reading

SKILL BOOK 3

Long Vowel Sounds

Frank C. Laubach
Elizabeth Mooney Kirk
Robert S. Laubach

Linguistic Consultant: Jeanette D. Macero

ISBN 0-88336-903-6

© 1982
New Readers Press
Publishing Division of Laubach Literacy International
Box 131, Syracuse, New York 13210

All rights reserved. No part of this book may be reproduced or transmitted in any form or by any means, electronic or mechanical, including photocopying, recording, or by any information storage and retrieval system, without permission in writing from the publisher.

Printed in the United States of America

Edited by Caroline Blakely and Kay Koschnick
Designed and illustrated by Chris Steenwerth

20 19 18 17 16 15 14 13

Lesson 1

ā, ē, ī, ō, ū, ȳ, (ī)

	paper	p ā p er ā	paper
	we	w ē ē	we
	I	ī ī	I
	go	g ō ō	go
	music	m ū z i c ū	music
	my	m ȳ ȳ (ī)	my

or

YORK ST.	York	Y or k or	York

My Class

Jason (Jāson)	Carla (Carlu)	class	listen	(lisen)
David (Dāvid)	Lopez (Lōpez)	snack	write	(rīt)
		study	sentence	(sentens)

I am Jason Hunt. I work at a market on River Street. I go to class after work. I have some paper. The paper is for my class.

After work, I will pick up my friend David Miller. He works at a factory on York Street. I will pick up David at the factory. We will go to class in my car.

Carla Lopez works at a music shop on York Street. We will pick up Carla at the music shop. She will go to class with us.

We will study hard in class. We will study the lesson. We will write on the paper. We will write sentences. We will write letters to friends. Ms. Smith will help us write sentences. She will help us write letters.

After class, Carla, David, and I will go for a snack. We will go to Fran's Snack Shop. It is on York Street. We can get a quick snack at Fran's. We can listen to music. We can have a snack and listen to music.

From the snack shop, we will go to Garden Street. Carla lives on Garden Street. Then David and I will go to First Street. David lives at 917 First Street. I live at 942 First Street.

I work hard. I study hard. But I have fun.

Story Checkup

story, missing

The names in this story are:

Jason Hunt David Miller Carla Lopez Ms. Smith

Write the name.

1. Who works at the market? _____
2. Who works at the factory? _____
3. Who works at the music shop? _____
4. Who has a car? _____
5. Who lives on Garden Street? _____
6. Who lives on First Street?

   _____ and _____

7. Who will go to class with Jason?

   _____ and _____

8. Who will help them write? _____

Write the missing word.

live
lives

1. David and Jason _____ on First Street.

work
works

2. I _____ at the market.

work
works

3. Carla _____ at a music shop.

write
writes

4. We _____ on the paper.

read (rēd)

ham	milk	I'll (Īll)	salad (salud)
hamburger	drink	sandwich	coffee (coffē)

Jason, Carla, and David were in Fran's Snack Shop. Fran hurried to them.

Fran asked, "What will you have?"

Jason said, "I'll have a ham sandwich."
Carla said, "I'll have an egg salad sandwich."
David said, "I'll have a hamburger."

Fran asked Jason, "What will you have to drink?"
Jason said, "I'll have a glass of milk."

Fran asked Carla, "What will you have to drink?"
Carla said, "I'll have a cup of coffee."

Fran asked David, "What will you have to drink?"
David said, "I'll have a glass of milk."

bill	¢ (cent)	70¢	(seventy cents)
cost	$ (dollar)	$1.00	(one dollar)
		$1.70	(one dollar and seventy cents)

Sandwiches

Ham sandwich $2.00
Egg salad sandwich $1.00
Hamburger $1.70

Drinks

Milk . . . . . 70¢
Coffee . . . . . 50¢

Write the missing numbers with $ or ¢.

Jason got a ham sandwich.
The ham sandwich cost _____.
Jason got a glass of milk.
The milk cost _____.
His bill was $2.70.

Carla got an egg salad sandwich.
The egg salad sandwich cost _____.
Carla got a cup of coffee.
The coffee cost _____.
Her bill was $1.50.

David got a hamburger.
The hamburger cost _____.
David got a glass of milk.
The milk cost _____.
His bill was $2.40.

Copy the word. Add -s or -es. What is the word?

egg eggs

dish dishes

1. glass Glasses
2. car cars
3. drink drinks
4. class classes
5. dress dresses
6. paper Papers
7. salad salads
8. box boxes
9. friend friends
10. sandwich sandwiches

Drop -s or -es. Write the word.

friends friend

dishes dish

1. cups cup
2. bills bill
3. classes class
4. words word
5. glasses glass
6. sentences Sentence
7. names name
8. kisses kisse
9. sandwiches Sandwich
10. shops shop

ā

paper

ā

	David	Dā vid	David
April 1 2 3 4 5 6 7 8 9 10 11 12 13 14 15 16 17 18 19 20 21 22 23 24 25 26 27 28 29 30	April	Ā pril	April
	baby	bā by	baby
	lady	lā dy	lady
	table	tā bul	table
	radio	rā dē ō	radio

Carla's Story

love (luv)	me (mē)	apartment (u part ment)
month (munth)	Rosa (Rō su)	baby-sitter (baby sit er)

My name is Carla Lopez. I live in an apartment on Garden Street. I have lived in this apartment for ten months.

I work at a music shop. I started work in April. I have worked at the music shop for six months.

After work, I go to class. I started the class in April. April was not a bad month! David was at the first class. David has helped me a lot in class. He and I are friends. David helps me with Rosa. He loves Rosa.

Rosa is my baby. She is two. My baby cannot go to work with me. She cannot go to class with me. A baby-sitter must look after her. Mrs. King is my baby-sitter. Mrs. King is a lady in my apartment building. This lady loves my baby. My baby loves her. I am happy that this lady is my baby-sitter.

It is after work. I have picked up Rosa from Mrs. King's apartment. Rosa is with me in the kitchen. Rosa is sitting at the table. She is singing. I am working at the table. I am starting dinner.

A radio is on the table. I am listening to the radio. The radio says that it is half past six. I must hurry. My friend David is coming to dinner.

Story Checkup

answer (an ser)

Answer with one or two words. Write the answer.

1. Who has worked at the music shop for six months?

   _____

2. Who has helped Carla in class? _____

3. When did Carla start the class? _____

4. Who is the baby-sitter? _____

5. What is the baby's name? _____

6. Who is coming to dinner? _____

Answer with *yes* or *no*. Write the answer.

1. Does Carla Lopez live on Garden Street? _____

2. Is David Carla's brother? _____

3. Can Rosa go to class with Carla? _____

4. Does Rosa love the baby-sitter? _____

5. Did Carla pick up Rosa after work? _____

6. Is Carla listening to the radio? _____

instant (in stant) potatoes (pu tā tōz) pat water (wot er)

Carla is getting dinner. She and David will have ham, salad, and potatoes for dinner. The potatoes are instant potatoes. This is on the box of instant potatoes.

	Water	Butter	Milk	Instant Potatoes
For 1 person	1 half cup	1 pat	1 quarter cup	1 half cup
For 2 persons	1 cup	2 pats	1 half cup	1 cup
For 4 persons	2 cups	4 pats	1 cup	2 cups

Put water, butter, and milk in a pan.
When the water gets hot, add instant potatoes.
Cover and let stand.

Fill in the numbers and words.

1. Carla is getting dinner for two persons.

   She puts 1 cup of water in a pan.

   She puts in 2 Pats of butter.

   She puts in 1 half cup of milk.

   When the water gets hot, she adds 1 cup of instant potatoes.

2. I have four persons in my family. For four persons,

   I will put 2 cups of water in a pan.

   I will put in 4 Pats of butter.

   I will put in 1 cup of milk.

   When the water gets hot, I will add 2 cups of instant potatoes.

Practice

practice (prac tis), say (sā), sound, syllable (sil u bul)

Say the words. Which word has the sound ā? Circle that word.

snack (snake)

1. baby happy
2. apple table
3. paper faster
4. name man
5. after April
6. Jason happen
7. Dan David
8. radio traffic

Look at the picture, and say the word.
Under the picture, write the number of syllables in the word.

1. _____

2. _____

3. _____

4. _____

5. _____

6. _____

7. _____

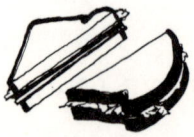

8. _____

Write the word.

baby
mother

1. Rosa is Carla's baby.

man
woman

2. The baby-sitter is a woman.

six
ten

3. The radio says it is half past six.

David
Jason

4. David is coming to dinner.

ham
fish

5. They will have ham for dinner.

Say the word. Write the number of syllables.

1. lady 2
2. hat 1
3. April 2
4. potato 3
5. that 1
6. baby 2
7. has 1
8. radio 2
9. paper 2
10. apartment 3
11. man 1
12. hamburger 3

ay = ā

day = dā

ay = ā

	pay	pay	pay
 May 1 2 3 4 5 6 7 8 9 10 11 12 13 14 15 16 17 18 19 20 21 22 23 24 25 26 27 28 29 30 31	May	May	May
	Kay	Kay	Kay
	Ray	Ray	Ray
	play	play	play
	away	u way	away

After Payday

rent	next	card	Mason	(Mā son)	today	(to day)
spent	last	check	hundred	(hun dred)	yesterday	(yes ter day)
had					payday	(pay day)

Today is the first day of May. Yesterday was payday. Yesterday was payday for Kay and Ray Mason. Their payday is the last day of the month. They got five hundred dollars.

The Masons are paying their bills today. Ray is looking at the bills. Kay is writing checks.

The Masons have to pay a lot of bills in May. They have to pay their rent today. The rent is for May. They have to pay the telephone bill for April. They have to pay the water bill for three months. They have to pay Kay's doctor bill. They have to pay some other bills.

Kay writes a check for the rent. She writes checks for the other bills.

Ray asks, "Have we spent the last cent?"

Kay laughs, "No, we have not spent the last cent. But we have spent a lot. Yesterday, we had five-hundred twenty-five dollars. Today, we have seventy-five dollars left."

"We can live on that," Ray says. "The next payday is May 15. But can we have any fun?"

Kay says, "Yes, we can play cards. Carla and David can come and play cards with us. It is fun to play cards."

Ray says, "We can have a little fun. But we can have a lot of fun after the next payday. We will have five hundred dollars. And we will not have many bills then. We can go away after the next payday. Let's go away the last three days in May."

"Yes, let's go away then," says Kay.

Story Checkup

short

Write a short *yes* or *no* answer.

Was yesterday the Masons' payday ? Yes, it was.

1. Do the Masons have to pay a lot of bills? _____
2. Does Ray write the checks? _____
3. Have the Masons spent a lot? _____
4. Have they spent their last cent? _____
5. Is their next payday April 15? _____
6. Can the Masons play cards? _____
7. Do the Masons plan to go away in May? _____

bank your

On April 29, the Masons had $25.00 in the bank. On April 30, they put $500.00 in the bank. Then they had $525.00 in the bank. They had to pay their bills with that $525.00.

Today is May 1. Kay writes a check for the rent. This is the check.

Ray Mason
Kay Mason

301

May 1 19 86

Pay to Ellen Smith $ 225.00

Two hundred twenty-five and 00/100 DOLLARS

First City Bank
Garden City, CA

Kay Mason

Today is May 15. You are paying your bills. You have a bill from Dr. John Black. The bill is for $25.00. Write the check to pay your bill. Write your name on the check.

1264

_____ 19____

Pay to _____ $ _____

_____ DOLLARS

_____

Practice

Say the words. Which word has the sound ā? Circle that word.

day dad

1.	ran	Ray	5.	Pam	pay
2.	play	plan	6.	Kay	Cal
3.	any	away	7.	say	Sam
4.	May	many	8.	valley	today

Copy the word. Add *-ing*.
Then write the words in the sentences.

pick picking

Carla is picking up Rosa.

play _____ go _____

pay _____ start _____

1. I am _____ to class.

2. Carla is _____ dinner.

3. The Masons are _____ their bills.

4. Kay and Ray are _____ cards.

Homework

Write the missing word.

1. Yesterday was _____ for the Masons.
2. They got five _____ dollars.
3. The Masons are _____ their bills.
4. Kay is writing _____.
5. They have _____ dollars left.
6. The next payday is _____ 15.

Say the word. Write the number of syllables.

1. pay	_____	8. hundred	_____
2. paying	_____	9. next	_____
3. go	_____	10. playing	_____
4. play	_____	11. cards	_____
5. yesterday	_____	12. going	_____
6. today	_____	13. telephone	_____
7. rent	_____	14. day	_____

ai = ā

paint = pānt

ai = ā

	nail	nail	nail
	Gail	Gail	Gail
	paid	paid	paid
	hair	hair	hair
	chair	chair	chair
	stairs	stairz	stairs

Painting

shall	ever (ev er)	OK	(ō kay)
gray	never (nev er)	landlady	(land lady)

Gail Fisher and Jason Hunt planned to get married. They rented an apartment. They said to the landlady, "We will paint the kitchen. Will you pay for the paint?"

The landlady asked, "Have you ever painted a kitchen?"

Jason said, "No, I have never painted a kitchen. But I have painted stairs."

"OK," said the landlady. "You get the paint and some nails. You can fix the stairs first. Then you can paint the stairs and your kitchen. I'll pay you for the paint and the nails."

"Shall we paint the kitchen red?" asked Jason.

"No, let's not," said Gail. "Let's paint it pink. What color shall we paint the stairs?"

Jason said, "Let's paint the stairs gray. Shall we get some black paint? We can paint the table and chairs black."

"OK," said Gail.

Jason and Gail got the paint and the nails. Gail paid for them.

The landlady paid Gail for the pink and gray paint. She paid Gail for the nails.

Gail and Jason got ready to paint. Gail covered her hair.

"Have you ever had paint in your hair?" Jason asked.

Gail said, "No, I never have. I cover my hair when I paint. Shall we paint the table and chairs first?"

Jason said, "No, let's not. Let's paint the kitchen first. Then you can paint the table and chairs. I have never painted chairs. I'll fix the stairs and paint them."

Story Checkup

Write a short *yes* or *no* answer.

Has Jason ever painted a kitchen? No, he has not.

1. Have Gail and Jason rented an apartment? _____
2. Will they paint the kitchen red? _____
3. Has Jason ever painted chairs? _____
4. Did Gail cover her hair? _____
5. Did the landlady pay for the gray paint? _____
6. Did the landlady pay for the black paint? _____
7. Will Jason paint the table and chairs? _____

quart (quort) gallon (gal un)

$3 a quart
$10 a gallon

$4 a quart
$14 a gallon

$5 a quart
$18 a gallon

Write the missing number with $.

1. Gail and Jason got one gallon of pink paint.

   They paid _____ for it.

2. They got one gallon of gray paint.

   They paid _____ for it.

3. They got two quarts of black paint.

   They paid _____ for it.

4. The pink, gray, and black paint cost _____.

5. Their landlady paid them for the pink and gray paint.

   She paid them _____.

Practice

Say the words. Which word has the sound ā? Circle that word.

1.	paint	pan	5.	chair	Chan
2.	starts	stairs	6.	neck	nail
3.	Gail	girl	7.	hair	has
4.	pack	paid	8.	gray	grass

Copy the word. Add *-ed*.
Then write the words in the sentences.

play played

They played cards.

paint _____ ask _____

rent _____ cover _____

1. Jason and Gail _____ an apartment.
2. Jason has never _____ a kitchen.
3. Gail _____ her hair.
4. "Shall we paint the kitchen red?" _____ Jason.

Homework

Answer with a sentence.

1. What did Gail and Jason rent? _____

_____

2. What color will they paint the kitchen? _____

_____

3. Who will paint the stairs? _____

_____

4. Who will paint the chairs? _____

_____

Say the word. Write the number of syllables.

1. paint _____
2. painted _____
3. stairs _____
4. chairs _____
5. rented _____
6. asked _____
7. covered _____
8. landlady _____
9. paid _____
10. never _____

a–e = ā

cake = cāk

a–e = ā

	bake	bake bāk	bake
	take	take tāk	take
	Jane	Jane Jān	Jane
	ate	ate āt	ate
	plate	plate plāt	plate
	care	care cār	care

The Wedding

yet	came	where (whare)	church	wedding (wed ing)
still	gave	there (thare)	party (par ty)	yourself (your self)

Jason and Gail got married in Gail's church. Jason's family and friends came to the wedding. Gail's family and friends came. After the wedding, there was a party. The party was in a building next to the church.

At the party, there was a big wedding cake. It was on a pretty glass plate. There were little sandwiches, coffee, and other drinks. There were paper plates and cups.

"Take a plate and help yourself to sandwiches," said Gail's sister Jane. "And help yourself to drinks."

"May I have some cake?" asked Jason's little brother Sam.

"No, not yet," said Jane. "Jason and Gail have to cut the cake first."

"Where are they?" asked Sam.

"They are still in the church," Jane said. "Gail's uncle is still taking pictures of them. He will take a picture of the wedding cake when they cut it."

"Who baked the wedding cake?" asked Carla.

Jane said, "Jason's mother baked it. She bakes many wedding cakes."

Just then, Jason and Gail came from the church. They cut the wedding cake. Jason gave Gail some cake, and she gave him some. They ate their cake.

Jason's little brother said, "I have not had any cake yet." Jason gave him some.

Gail said to the others, "Come and help yourself to some cake." Their family ate cake. Their friends ate cake.

Jason said to Gail, "Let's go!"

Jason's little brother said, "Where are you going?"

"Away," Jason said.

"You cannot go yet," said Gail's father. "I still have not kissed my little girl." He kissed Gail and said, "Take care of her, Jason."

Jason said, "Yes, Dad, I will take care of her. And she will take care of me."

Story Checkup

right (rīt)

Circle the letter of the right answer.

Who got married?

(a.) Jason and Gail

b. Carla and David

1. Where was the wedding?
   a. in Gail's church
   b. in Carla's apartment
2. Where was the party?
   a. in the church
   b. in a building next to the church
3. Where was the wedding cake?
   a. on a paper plate
   b. on a glass plate
4. Who was taking pictures?
   a. Gail's father
   b. Gail's uncle

frame	much
date	dear (dēr)

Gail and Jason got many wedding gifts. Some of the gifts were glasses, plates, curtains, a chair, a table, a rug, a clock radio, and a picture frame.

Gail is writing thank you letters for the gifts. First, she writes the date. She puts the date at the top of the letter. She starts the letter with the word *Dear* and the person's name.

May 21, 1986

Dear Carla,

Thank you very much for the picture frame. Jason and I think that it is very pretty. We will put a wedding picture in the frame.

Thank you very much for coming to the wedding. You are a dear friend.

With love,
Gail

1. What is the date on the letter? _____

2. Who is the letter to? _____

3. What was the gift? _____

4. Who is Gail's dear friend? _____

Practice

Say the words. Circle the words with the sound ā.

	bake	back	gave	bank
1.	came	cake	gave	bank
2.	gray	Gail	girl	care
3.	check	chair	hair	Chan
4.	Sam	Ray	Jane	Ann
5.	ham	plate	play	class

Copy the word but not the *e*. Add *-ing*.
Then write the words in the sentences.

have having

They are having a party.

take _____ give _____

bake _____ write _____

1. Jason's mother is _____ a cake.
2. Gail's uncle is _____ pictures.
3. Gail is _____ a letter.
4. Jane is _____ Sam some cake.

Homework

Answer with a sentence.

1. Where was the wedding? _____

_____

2. Who baked the wedding cake? _____

_____

3. Who cut the wedding cake? _____

_____

4. Who gave Sam some cake? _____

_____

Say the word. Write the number of syllables.

1. baked _____
2. wedding _____
3. yourself _____
4. came _____
5. kissed _____
6. much _____
7. taking _____
8. baking _____
9. party _____
10. writing _____

More Reading with ā

paper	cake	paint	day
ā	a-e	ai	ay

1. Dinner for Two

TV

David came to Carla's apartment for dinner. When he came in, he kissed Carla. He said, "Your hair looks very pretty."

"Thank you, dear," said Carla. "My landlady cut my hair yesterday."

"Where is Rosa?" asked David.

"She is in bed," Carla said. "Dinner is ready. Help yourself to coffee, and I'll drink milk."

David and Carla ate their dinner. They had ham, potatoes, and salad.

After dinner, they had coffee and watched TV.

2. The Card Party

Carla and David came to the Masons' apartment. They came to play cards. They did not bring Carla's baby with them. The baby-sitter was taking care of her.

Ray Mason put four chairs at the card table. The friends played cards and listened to music on the radio. After they played cards, they ate some cake. They had coffee with their cake.

"Kay, did you bake this cake?" asked David.

"No," said Kay. "Ray baked it today."

"Your plates are very pretty," Carla said.

"Thank you very much," said Kay. "My mother gave them to me."

After they ate their cake, David and Carla thanked the Masons and left.

3. Three Days at Snake River

The Masons' payday was May 15. They put their checks in the bank and paid their bills. They went away for the last three days in May.

Kay and Ray went to Snake River. They had fun there. They fished in the river. They played in the water. They picked up pretty rocks.

When they came back, Ray said, "We spent a hundred dollars. But it was fun."

4. In the Kitchen

It was a month after the Hunts' wedding. Gail and Jason were sitting in their kitchen. They were having a snack. There were some sandwiches and a quart of milk on the table.

The landlady came up the stairs. Jason said, "Come in and have a snack with us."

"No, thanks," she said. "But may I look at your kitchen? I am happy that you painted it pink. I have a gallon of paint. Will you paint my kitchen? I will pay you for it."

"OK," said Jason. "We will paint it next month."

Lesson 7

we

ē

ē

ee = ē

see = sē

ee = ē

	he	hē	he
	tree	tree	tree
	wheel	wheel	wheel
	teeth	teeth	teeth
	sleep	sleep	sleep

Lee's Lesson

Lee	need	be	late	again (u gen)	wasn't	(wuz unt)
Green	beer	it's	face (fase)	angry (ang gry)	didn't	(did unt)

Mrs. Green was in bed, but she wasn't sleeping. "Where is Lee?" she was thinking. "It's half past three."

Lee was 16. He had a job after class. He had his first car.

Mrs. Green heard a car. When Lee came in, she got up. "Where were you?" she yelled. "It's half past three. Were you drinking beer?"

"No, Mother," said Lee. "I wasn't drinking beer. I was just playing cards with my friends."

Mrs. Green said, "I cannot sleep when you come in late. You need to be in bed. You need your sleep."

"OK," said Lee. "Let's go to bed."

"What is that?" his mother said. "Do I see a cut on your face? Yes, I *do* see a cut."

"It's just a little cut," Lee said. "I went to sleep at the wheel. I didn't see the tree. My car hit the tree. My face hit the wheel. But I wasn't going fast. And I wasn't drinking beer!"

Mrs. Green said, "Did you hit your teeth on the wheel?"

"No, I didn't hit my teeth," Lee said. "My teeth are OK, and my face will be OK. My car still runs, but the tree looks bad."

Lee said, "Do not be angry with me, Mother. I have had a hard lesson. I will not be late again."

"I was very angry," said Mrs. Green. "And I am still angry. Do not be late again, or I will take your car away."

"But, Mother, I need my car to go to work," said Lee.

"Then do not be late again," she said. "And you will have to pay for that tree."

Story Checkup

Circle the letter of the right answer.

1. Did Lee have a car?
   a. Yes, he had a car.
   b. No, he didn't have a car.
2. Was Mrs. Green sleeping?
   a. Yes, she was sleeping.
   b. No, she wasn't sleeping.
3. Did Lee hit his teeth?
   a. Yes, he hit his teeth.
   b. No, he didn't hit his teeth.
4. Was Mrs. Green angry?
   a. Yes, she was angry.
   b. No, she wasn't angry.
5. Is Lee's face cut?
   a. Yes, it's cut a little.
   b. No, it's not cut.

1 one	11 eleven (ē lev en)	10 ten
2 two	12 twelve	20 twenty
3 three	13 thirteen	30 thirty
4 four	14 fourteen	40 forty
5 five	15 fifteen	50 fifty
6 six	16 sixteen	60 sixty
7 seven	17 seventeen	70 seventy
8 eight (āt)	18 eighteen	80 eighty
9 nine (nīn)	19 nineteen	90 ninety
10 ten	20 twenty	100 one hundred

Write the number.

nine	9	thirteen	13	seventy-seven	77
nineteen	_____	thirty	_____	ninety-nine	_____
ninety	_____	fifteen	_____	sixty-six	_____
eight	_____	fifty	_____	eighty-eight	_____
eighteen	_____	fourteen	_____	fifty-five	_____
eighty	_____	forty	_____	forty-four	_____
eleven	_____	sixteen	_____	thirty-three	_____
seven	_____	sixty	_____	thirteen	_____
seventeen	_____	eleven	_____	fifteen	_____

Practice

Say the words. Which word has the sound ē? Circle that word.

1.	Ned	need	5.	bed	beer
2.	well	wheel	6.	teeth	tent
3.	see	send	7.	sleep	seven
4.	Lee	let	8.	ten	teen

Say the word. Write the two words that it comes from.

let's let us

1. it's _____ _____
2. wasn't _____ _____
3. didn't _____ _____
4. I'll _____ _____

Fill in the word: *let's, it's, wasn't, didn't, I'll.*

1. _____ not a bad cut.
2. Lee _____ see the tree.
3. He _____ drinking beer
4. _____ pay you for the paint.
5. _____ not go to the party.

Homework

Answer with a sentence.

1. Who was angry? _____

_____

2. Who went to sleep at the wheel? _____

_____

3. What did Lee's car hit? _____

_____

4. Who will have to pay for the tree? _____

_____

Say the word. Write the number of syllables.

1. seventeen _____
2. nineteen _____
3. nine _____
4. fourteen _____
5. sleeping _____
6. fifty _____
7. drinking _____
8. yelled _____
9. better _____
10. need _____

ea = ē

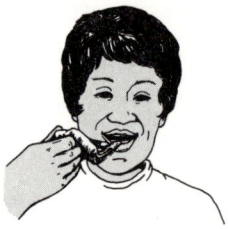

eat = ēt

ea = ē

	meat	meat	meat
	meal	meal	meal
	beans	beanz	beans
	tea	tea	tea
	teacher	teach er	teacher
	please	pleaz	please

The Class Party

each	eaten (eat en)	cheese (cheez)	best
cheap		people (pē pul)	something (some thing)

Carla's class is having a dinner party. There will be a big meal.

Each person brings something to eat. Carla brings beans. David brings a green salad. Jason and Gail bring baked potatoes. The Masons bring apples and cheese. Other people bring something to eat.

Ms. Smith, the teacher, brings the meat. The meat wasn't cheap. Each person helped to pay for the meat.

There are eighteen people at the party. They are having fun and eating a big meal.

"Please pass the meat," says Ray. "I have not eaten any meat for three days."

Kay says, "That is right. Meat is not cheap. For many meals, we have eggs, beans, or cheese. They are pretty cheap."

The teacher says, "Please pass the beans. Carla's beans are the best beans that I have ever eaten."

Jason says, "This is the best salad that I have ever eaten."

The people at the party eat their dinner. Then Ray passes apples and cheese. The teacher brings coffee and tea to the table. She asks each person, "Will you have coffee or tea?"

"I'll have tea, please," says Gail. "And Jason will have coffee."

"This is the best party that we have ever had," says Carla. "Let's have another one."

Story Checkup

Write a short answer.

1. Who is having a party? _____
2. What does Carla bring? _____
3. What do Jason and Gail bring? _____
4. Who brings the meat? _____
5. Who pays for the meat? _____

Read this list of words.
Then write one of the words in each sentence.

eat, meal, tea, please, cheap

1. The people are eating a big _____.
2. Each person brings something to _____.
3. _____ pass the meat.
4. Will you have coffee or _____ ?
5. The meat wasn't _____.

ad

Green Hills Market

Green Beans
3 cans for **$1.00**

Fresh Baked
BREAD
79¢

Ham $1.39

Hamburger **$1.69**

Cheese **$2.79**

MILK
Quart **55¢**
Half gallon **98¢**

Butter
$1.75

100
Tea Bags
$1.79

Apple Jelly 88¢

Instant
COFFEE
$2.89

Large
EGGS 89¢

Instant Potatoes **99¢**

Please read this ad. Then write the answers.

1. Hamburger is in the ad. What other meat is there? _____

2. What three things to drink are in this ad?

   _____

3. What does a quart of milk cost? _____

4. What does a half gallon of milk cost? _____

5. What does the bread cost? _____

6. What does a box of 100 tea bags cost? _____

7. What do three cans of green beans cost? _____

8. What does a jar of instant coffee cost? _____

Practice

Say the words. Which word has the sound ē? Circle the word.

1.	it	eat	5.	meat	men
2.	tea	ten	6.	plate	please
3.	dark	dear	7.	bill	meal
4.	red	read	8.	bean	best

Copy the word. Add *-r* or *-er*.
Then write one of the words in each sentence.

farm farmer

Mr. Arthur is a farmer.

write writer

Ann is a writer.

teach _____

bake _____

paint _____

read _____

1. Ms. Smith is Carla's _____.
2. The _____ is painting the apartment.
3. The _____ is baking bread.
4. She can read the story quickly.

   She is a fast _____.

Homework

Answer with a sentence.

1. What do the Masons bring? _____

_____

2. Who brings a salad? _____

_____

3. What does Ms. Smith bring to the table? _____

_____

_____

Say the word. Write the number of syllables.

1. tea _____
2. people _____
3. eat _____
4. something _____
5. eaten _____
6. baked _____
7. baking _____
8. baker _____
9. read _____
10. reader _____
11. teacher _____
12. potatoes _____

Lesson 9

Pete = Pēt

e–e = ē

e–e = ē

ey = ē

key = kē

ey = ē

	Steve	Steve	Steve
	these	theze	these
	evening	eve ning	evening
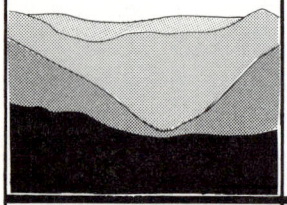	valley	val ey	valley
	money	mun ey	money

Steve's Job

clean	keep	make	repair (rē pair)
teach	week	save	Saturday (Sat ur day)
	here	place (plase)	

Steve is seventeen. He has a job at Pete's Valley Repair Shop. Pete repairs radios, TVs, and other things.

Steve's job is to keep the place clean. He keeps the shop clean. He keeps the stairs clean. Pete is teaching him to repair radios. Next, Pete will teach him to repair TVs.

Steve works from six to nine in the evening. And he works on Saturday.

Steve does not make much money at his job. He makes $60 a week. Steve saves some of his money. He has worked at the repair shop for six weeks. In six weeks, he has saved $120 dollars. He is saving his money to get a color TV.

One evening, Pete gives Steve some keys. "These are the keys to the shop," Pete says. "I will not be here on Saturday. You can take care of the place."

"OK," says Steve. "I will be here at eight on Saturday. I will take care of the place very well."

Pete says, "A lot of people will come in to pick up their things. These radios are ready. These TVs are ready. I was going to repair Mrs. Green's radio yesterday, but I didn't. You can fix it."

On Saturday, Mrs. Green comes in. Steve gives her the radio that he fixed. Other people come in. Steve gives them their things and takes their money.

That evening, Pete comes back. Steve says, "Here are your keys. Here is the money that I got today. I fixed Mrs. Green's radio, and she picked it up."

Pete says, "You can keep the money she gave you. You worked hard today."

Story Checkup

Write a short *yes* or *no* answer.

1. Is Steve fifteen? _____

2. Has Steve saved $120? _____

3. Did Pete work in the shop on Saturday? _____

4. Did Steve repair Mrs. Green's radio? _____

5. Is Pete teaching Steve to repair radios? _____

Read these five sentences. What happened first?
You will see a number 1 next to that sentence.
What happened next? Put a number 2 next to that sentence.
Put the right numbers next to the other sentences.

_____ Steve fixes Mrs. Green's radio.

__1__ Pete gives Steve some keys.

_____ Steve gives Mrs. Green the radio.

_____ Steve gives Pete the keys.

_____ That evening, Pete comes back.

second (sec und)	tax	labor (lā ber)
third	part	

PETE'S VALLEY REPAIR SHOP
332 Second Street
Garden City

Name Jane Fisher

Address 332 Third Street

Date April 16, 1986

For TV repair

Parts	$12.14
Labor	30.00
	42.14
Tax	2.32
	$44.46

Please read this bill. Then write short answers.

1. What is this bill for? _____
2. What do the parts cost? $ _____
3. What does the labor cost? $ _____
4. What is the tax? $ _____
5. Which costs more, the parts or the labor? _____
6. Which costs more, the parts or the tax? _____
7. What does Jane Fisher have to pay? $ _____
8. What is the date on the bill? _____
9. Is the repair shop on Second Street? _____
10. Does Jane Fisher live on Third Street? _____

Practice

Say the words. Circle the words with the sound ē.

1.	clean	class	please	last
2.	money	meat	key	month
3.	well	week	went	with
4.	these	here	her	this
5.	pet	Pete	teach	pick

Drop *-ing* or *-ed*. Write the word that is left.

1. keeping _____
2. painted _____
3. eating _____
4. played _____
5. drinking _____
6. reading _____
7. repaired _____
8. needed _____
9. paying _____
10. yelled _____
11. cleaned _____
12. teaching _____

Homework

Answer with a sentence.

1. Where does Steve work? _____

_____

2. What is Steve saving his money for? _____

_____

3. Who repaired Mrs. Green's radio? _____

_____

4. Who gave the keys to Steve? _____

_____

Say the word. Write the number of syllables.

1. cleaned _____
2. repaired _____
3. money _____
4. saved _____
5. seventeen _____
6. Saturday _____
7. week _____
8. yesterday _____
9. fixed _____
10. labor _____

Lesson 10

More Reading with ā and ē

paper	cake	paint		day
ā	a–e	ai		ay
we	Pete	eat	see	key
ē	e–e	ea	ee	ey

1. A Teenager Pays

teenager (teen āj er)

It was Saturday. Lee Green went to see the tree that he hit. When he got there, a woman was standing next to the tree. She looked angry. "Are you the teenager that hit my tree?" she asked.

"Yes, I am." said Lee. "I went to sleep at the wheel."

"You teenagers!" she yelled, and her face got red. "You do not care what you do! You drink beer! You go fast in your cars! You do not need cars!"

"I am a teenager," said Lee. "But I wasn't drinking beer. I wasn't going fast. And I do care. I came to pay for your tree."

"We cannot save this tree," said the woman. "It will not live. It will cost a hundred dollars to get another one."

"That is a lot of money," said Lee. "I can pay you twenty dollars today. I have a job. I can pay you twenty dollars a week."

The woman said, "I am happy that you came back. You are OK."

2. Pete's Story

team	hockey (hock ey)	Canada (Can u du)
year	player (play er)	

I am Pete. I run the repair shop on Second Street. Steve works for me in the evenings. He keeps the place clean. I am teaching him to repair things.

Let me tell you my story. I was a teenager in the 1940s. I lived with my mother in Canada. My father was dead. When I was nineteen, I got a job with a hockey team in Canada. I was going to be a big hockey player and make a lot of money.

My mother left Canada and came back to Garden City. Then she got sick. She needed me to take care of her. I came to Garden City. I got a job at a TV factory. I started repairing TVs. I repaired them in the evening at the kitchen table.

Many years passed. My mother did not get well. I never went back to my hockey team. After fourteen years, I started my repair shop.

When I think back, I am not very happy. I was going to be a big hockey player. Many people were going to see me play. I was going to make a lot of money. These things never happened.

But I am happy with the hockey team that I have today. There are fifteen teenagers on my team. I am teaching these boys to play hockey. They think that I am the best hockey player there is.

"Not the best," I tell them. "But I still have my teeth, and a lot of hockey players do not. And I have you. We will be the best hockey team in the valley. And next year we will play in Canada."

Lesson 11

I

i

ī

i–e = ī

time

i–e = ī

	ride	rīde rīd	ride
	drive	drīve drīv	drive
	driver	drīv er	driver
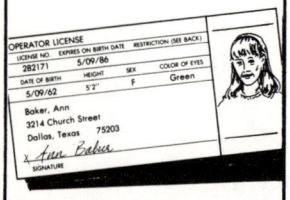	license	lī sens	license
	bicycle	bī sic ul	bicycle

Getting a Driver's License

eye (ī)	same	test	written (rit en)
if	state	tester (test er)	permit (per mit)

Who needs a driver's license? What do I have to do to get one? Do I need license plates? The answers are not the same in each of the 50 states. But the answers are the same in many states.

You need a license to drive a car. You need a license to drive a truck. You do not need a license to ride a bicycle.

You must have license plates for your car. You must have license plates for a truck. In some places, you have to have license plates for a bicycle. In other places, you do not have to have license plates for a bicycle.

You get license plates from the state that you live in. You get your driver's license from your state.

To get a driver's license, you must take tests. One test is an eye test. To take this test, you have to read letters on a chart. The eye test tells if you need glasses to drive.

Another test is a written test. If you do not pass the written test the first time, you must not drive. But you can take this test again.

If you pass the written test, you get a permit to drive. A permit is not a license. But with a permit, you can start driving. Another person must ride with you. That person must have a driver's license.

The last test is a driving test. You are ready to take it when you can drive well. A tester will ride with you. The tester tells you where to drive and when to turn. The tester watches your driving and parking.

If you pass the driving test, you will get a driver's license. Many people do not pass this test the first time. If you do not pass the first time, you can take the driving test again. You can take it again and again.

Story Checkup

Circle *yes* or *no*.

1. Do you need a license to ride a bicycle? Yes No
2. Do you have to take tests to get a driver's license? Yes No
3. If you do not pass the written test, can you take it again? Yes No
4. Do you have to take an eye test to get a driver's license? Yes No
5. Do you have to take a test to get license plates? Yes No
6. Is a permit a license? Yes No
7. Can you take the driving test two times? Yes No
8. Do you have a driver's license? Yes No

birth	Dallas (Dal us)	zip code	(cōd)
sex	Texas (Tex us)	application	(ap li cā shun)

State of Texas
Application for Driver's License

Baker — Ann
Last name — First name

Date of birth: May 9, 1962 (Month/Day/Year) Sex: ☐ M ☒ F Eye color: Green

Address: 3214 Church Street
Number and Street

Dallas — Texas — 75203
City — State — Zip code

This is part of an application for a driver's license. Read the application, and write short answers.

1. What is this person's first name? _____
2. What is this person's last name? _____
3. Which box did this person mark for Sex? _____
4. Is this person a man or a woman? _____
5. What is her date of birth? _____
6. What is her street address in Dallas? _____
7. Is Texas a city or a state? _____
8. What is Ann's zip code? _____
9. What is your sex? Put an X in one box. ☐ M ☐ F
10. What is the year of your birth? _____

Practice

Say the words. Circle the words with the sound ī.

1.	ride	drive	ring	sick
2.	I	if	eye	first
3.	driving	living	driver	river
4.	fit	time	license	with
5.	building	bicycle	written	write

Copy the word. Add *-r* or *-er*.
Then write one of the words in each sentence.

ride _____ drive _____

test _____ play _____

1. A bicycle _____ does not need a license.
2. The _____ will ride with you when you take the driving test.
3. The _____ of a car must have a license.
4. Pete is a hockey _____.

Write short answers.

1. What is your first name? _____
2. What is your last name? _____
3. What is your street address?

   _____
4. What is the name of your state? _____
5. What is your zip code? _____
6. Do you have a driver's license? _____

Say the word. Write the number of syllables.

1. driver _____
2. bicycle _____
3. written _____
4. tester _____
5. ride _____
6. license _____
7. state _____
8. letters _____
9. glasses _____
10. application _____

i–e = ī

time

i–e = ī

	Mike	Mike Mīk	Mike
	like	like līk	like
MILE 4 4	mile	mile mīl	mile
	smile	smile smīl	smile
	wife	wife wīf	wife
	nice	nise nīs	nice

Running

White	tired	(tīrd)	race	(rase)	husband	(huz bund)
while	retired	(rē tīrd)	been	(bin)	breakfast	(brek fust)
	every	(ev er y)			sometimes	(some times)

Fran White is retired. Fran has been retired for three years. Her husband Mike has been retired for five years. These days, the Whites have a lot of time. The Whites have time to do things that they like.

Fran likes to run. Every day, she gets up at five and runs. She is getting ready for a big race. It is a mile race for retired women.

Fran must run five miles every day. Then she will not get tired in the mile race.

Fran has been running every day for three years. Her doctor said that it was OK. At first, Fran did not run very far or very fast. Every week, she ran a little more.

Sometimes, Fran runs in the park. Sometimes, she runs in the street. Today, Fran is running in the park. It is a nice day. People in the park smile at Fran. Fran smiles back at them.

While his wife runs, Mike makes breakfast. He likes to make breakfast while his wife is not in the kitchen.

When Fran comes back, breakfast is ready. Her husband smiles and says, "Is it a nice day?"

"Yes," says his wife. "It is a very nice day."

While they are eating, Mike looks at his wife. "Are you tired, dear?" he asks. "Sometimes, you get very tired."

"Well, I didn't get tired today," Fran says to her husband. "And I am getting fast. I think I am ready for the mile race."

Story Checkup

Circle the letter of the right answer.

1. What does Fran do every day when she gets up?
   a. run
   b. makes breakfast
   c. goes for a drive
2. What is Fran getting ready for?
   a. the five-mile race
   b. the one-mile race
   c. the driving test
3. What time does Fran get up?
   a. at six
   b. at five
   c. at seven
4. What does Mike do while his wife runs?
   a. runs with her
   b. goes to work
   c. makes breakfast

price (prise)	bus
sign (sīn)	age (aje)

In some places, retired people can get things for cheaper prices. At the age of 62 or 65, you can get these cheaper prices. You can ride the bus cheaper. You can get glasses cheaper. You can get many other things cheaper.

To get these cheaper prices, you need a permit. To get a permit, you have to fill in an application.

Here is an application for a bus permit. Fill it in for Mike White. He lives at 1400 Third Street in Dallas, Texas. His zip code is 75210. His date of birth is April 12, 1915. Do not sign your name. Sign his name. Give his age.

City Bus
Application for Retired Person's Permit

_____
Last Name First Name

Address: _____
Number and Street

_____
City State Zip Code

Date of Birth: _____ Age: _____ Sex: ☐M ☐F
Month Day Year

_____
Sign Here

Practice

Say the words. Circle the words with the sound ī.

1.	Miller	mile	wife	with
2.	Mike	milk	Smith	smile
3.	while	will	tired	third
4.	neck	nice	like	lift
5.	price	white	pick	which

Copy the word. Add *-d* or *-ed*.
Then write one of the words in each sentence.

retire _____ sign _____

smile _____ like _____

1. Fran has been _____ for three years.
2. Mike _____ at his wife.
3. Mike _____ the application.
4. Fran _____ to run in the park.

Drop the *-e* and add *-ing*. Write the word.

1. smile _____
2. retire _____
3. like _____
4. drive _____
5. ride _____

Homework

Write short answers.

1. What is Fran's last name? _____
2. What is her husband's first name? _____
3. Did the doctor say that it was OK for Fran to run? _____
4. Did Fran run very far at first? _____
5. What does Mike make while Fran runs? _____
6. Does Fran sometimes get tired from running? _____
7. Does Mike run with Fran? _____
8. Does Fran think that she is ready for the mile race? _____

Say the word. Write the number of syllables.

1. sometimes _____
2. every _____
3. breakfast _____
4. age _____
5. today _____
6. nice _____
7. cheaper _____
8. permit _____
9. husband _____
10. race _____

Lesson 13

my = mī

ȳ = ī

ȳ = ī

ie = ī

tie = tī

ie = ī

	cry cried	crȳ cried	cry cried
	dry dried	drȳ dried	dry dried
	try tried	trȳ tried	try tried
	fly	flȳ	fly
	die	die	die

A Brother Dies

by	feel	line
why	air	o'clock (u clock)

One day, Mike got up to make breakfast. It was time for Fran to run, but she was not running. She was sitting next to the telephone. She was crying. Fran tried to dry her eyes when Mike came in.

"Why have you been crying?" Mike asked.

"My brother Tom has died," said Fran. "His wife just telephoned me. She said that he died in his sleep." Fran started to cry again.

Mike tried to make Fran feel better. "There, there, dear," he said. "Cry. You will feel better if you cry."

"He was just 55," Fran cried. "Why did he have to die? Why?"

"Try to think of the happy times that you had with him," said Mike. "Then you will feel better."

Fran cried and cried. Then she dried her eyes. "Ellen will need us," she said. "We must fly there today if we can. I'll start packing while you telephone the air line."

Mike telephoned the air line. "The air line says that we can fly at half past nine," he said to Fran. "We must be there by nine o'clock. Can we be there by nine?"

"We can be ready if we hurry." Fran said. "Tell the air line that we will be there by nine o'clock."

Fran started packing. "Where is your black tie?" she asked Mike. "You will need that tie."

"Here is my black tie," Mike said. "Let me help you. We will save time if I help you."

The Whites packed their bags. From time to time, Fran stopped to dry her eyes. But she and Mike were ready to fly by nine o'clock.

Story Checkup

Answer with the name of a person in the story.

1. Who died in his sleep? _____
2. Who telephoned Fran? _____
3. Who was Ellen? _____
4. Who was Tom's sister? _____
5. Who was Fran's husband? _____
6. Who was Mike's wife? _____

Read these six sentences.
What happened first? You will see a number 1 next to that sentence.
What happened next? Put a number 2 next to that sentence.
Put the right numbers next to the other sentences.

_____ Fran answered the telephone.

_____ Ellen telephoned to Fran.

_____ Mike got up to make breakfast.

__1__ Tom died in his sleep.

_____ The Whites were ready to fly by nine.

_____ Mike telephoned the air line.

a.m.	Monday (Mun day)	service (ser vis)
p.m.	Friday (Frī day)	

When Fran's brother died, this story was in the *King City Times*. Read the story, and write short answers.

King City Times, Friday, April 11, 1986

Tom J. Roberts

Tom J. Roberts, 55, of 162 Green Street, died at 4:00 a.m. today. He died in his sleep at his apartment.

Mr. Roberts worked at the Hill Bicycle Shop for 25 years.

He left his wife, Mrs. Ellen Smith Roberts; two sons, Sam of Bell Gardens and John of Apple Valley; and one sister, Fran Roberts White of Dallas, Texas.

Services will be Monday at 2:30 p.m. at the Little Church in the Valley.

1. Who died? _____
2. Where did he live? _____
3. Mr. Roberts died on Friday. What was the date? _____
4. What time on Friday did he die? _____
5. Where did he work? _____
6. Who is his wife? _____
7. Who are his sons? _____
8. Who is the dead man's sister? _____
9. Where does she live? _____
10. What time are the church services on Monday? _____
11. What will the date be on Monday? _____
12. Where will the services be? _____

Practice

change (chānj)

Say the words. Circle the words with the sound ī.

1.	cry	city	by	baby
2.	my	dry	play	windy
3.	any	try	eye	tie
4.	puppy	die	why	way
5.	cried	angry	line	nine

Read the word. Change the *y* to *i*, and add *-es*.
Write the *-es* word in List 1.

Read the word again. Change the *y* to *i*, and add *-ed*.
Write the *-ed* word in List 2.

	List 1	List 2
cry	cries	cried
1. dry	_____	_____
2. try	_____	_____
3. carry	_____	_____
4. hurry	_____	_____
5. marry	_____	_____

Homework

Fill in the missing word or number.

1. _____ got up to make breakfast.
2. Tom was just _____ when he died.
3. Tom died in his _____.
4. Mike will need his black _____.
5. The Whites were ready by _____ o'clock.

Drop *-ing*, *-d*, or *-ed*. Write the word that is left.

trying try

1. crying _____
2. flying _____
3. drying _____
4. packing _____
5. died _____
6. tied _____
7. started _____
8. telephoned _____

igh = ī

night = nīt

igh = ī

	high	high	high
	light	light	light
	flight	flight	flight
	right	right	right
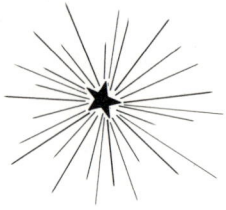	bright	bright	bright
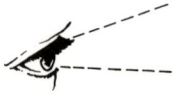	sight	sight	sight

A Night Flight from China

find	(fīnd)	child	(chīld)	I'm	(Īm)	sky	
behind	(bē hīnd)	China	(Chī nu)			sad	

My name is Lee Chan. I am on a night flight. I'm high in the sky. The night is dark. But the bright lights of my city are still in sight. The bright lights of China are still in sight.

I am going far away, and I feel sad. I'm on a night flight from China to the States. I'm going to the States to study.

From high in the sky, I look for the bright lights again. But they are not in sight. My city is far behind me.

I think of my family that I left behind. I left my wife and my child behind. I will not see them for four years. My child will be five by then. A child needs a father, but I will not be there. Am I doing the right thing?

What will I find in the States? Will I find a place to live? Will I find friends? Am I doing the right thing?

I must not think like that. It makes me sad. I *am* doing the right thing. I'll be OK in the States. I will study very hard. When I go back to China, I'll have a better job. I can take care of my family better. I can help China. I can make things better for my child and other children.

I will not be sad any more. From high in the sky, I see a bright light again. This time, it is the sun. Day has come.

Story Checkup

question (ques chun), himself (him self)

Answer each question with a sentence.

1. Where is Lee Chan from?

_____

2. Where is he going?

_____

3. Why is he going there?

_____

Lee asks himself some questions.
Write four questions that Lee asks himself.

1. _____

2. _____

3. _____

4. _____

gate	arrive (u rive)	cities (sit yz)
	depart (dē part)	timetable (time table)

Lee Chan has arrived in the States. He has to take another flight to Dallas, Texas. He will take a flight on Sun Air Line.

Here is the Sun Air Line timetable. The timetable has flights to and from many cities on it. On the left are flights that arrive from other cities. On the right are flights that go to other cities.

Study the timetable, and write the answers. When you tell the time, put *a.m.* or *p.m.* in the answer.

SUN AIR LINE

ARRIVE

Flight	From		Gate
740	Garden City	8:55 a.m.	2
406	Apple Valley	10:00 a.m.	5
505	Little Rock	12:40 p.m.	7
419	Dallas	2:00 p.m.	7
680	Sun Valley	2:45 p.m.	4

DEPART

Flight	To		Gate
740	Apple Valley	9:25 a.m.	2
406	Dallas	10:30 a.m.	5
505	Sun Valley	1:20 p.m.	7
670	Dallas	2:40 p.m.	7
530	Little Rock	3:15 p.m.	4

1. What time does Flight 740 arrive from Garden City? _____
2. What time does Flight 740 depart for Apple Valley? _____

   If you take this flight, which gate will you go to? _____
3. Two flights go to Dallas. Write the flight numbers. _____
4. Which flight to Dallas departs at 10:30 a.m.? _____
5. Which flight to Dallas departs at 2:40 p.m.? _____
6. Lee will take Flight 670. Which gate will he go to? _____

Practice

underline (under line)

Read the sentence. Underline each word with the sound ī.

I am on a night flight.

1. I left my wife and child behind.
2. My child will be five by then.
3. Am I doing the right thing?
4. I must not think like that.
5. The bright lights of China are still in sight.

Sometimes, two little words make one big word. Read the big word. Then write the two little words.

payday	pay	day
1. himself	_____	_____
2. yourself	_____	_____
3. something	_____	_____
4. sometimes	_____	_____
5. timetable	_____	_____
6. underline	_____	_____

Homework

Write three other words with *igh* that have the sound ī.

high _____ _____ _____

Write three other words with *y* that have the sound ī.

by _____ _____ _____

Write three other words with *i—e* that have the sound ī.

time _____ _____ _____

Change the *y* to *i*, and add *-es*.
Write one of the words in each sentence.

party _____ baby _____

city _____ story _____

factory _____ family _____

1. I like to read funny _____.
2. My class had two _____ this year.
3. The _____ are crying.
4. There are flights to many _____.
5. Many _____ live on this street.
6. The people in the _____ work hard.

More Reading with ā, ē, ī

paper	cake	paint		day
ā	a–e	ai		ay
we	Pete	eat	see	key
ē	e–e	ea	ee	ey
I	time	tie	night	my
ī	i–e	ie	igh	y

1. A Teenager Learns to Drive

learn (lern)

On the day that Jill was 16, she went to the state office building. She filled in an application for a driver's permit. She had to take a written test. The person that gave her the eye test said, "You must have your glasses on when you drive."

Jill got a driver's permit. Her mother started teaching her to drive. Jill learned to make left and right turns. She learned to watch for stop signs and red lights. She learned to watch for other traffic signs while she was driving. She learned to back up and to park.

"I'm ready to try the driving test," said Jill. But she did not pass the test the first time. The tester said that Jill did not stop at a stop sign. She had to take the driving test again. The second time, she passed. "I did it!" said Jill. "I have my driver's license!"

2. A Letter from Ellen Roberts

fine	wives (wīvz)	ago	(u gō)
life	myself (my self)	stories	(stor yz)

April 21

Dear Jane,

I have something sad to tell you. My husband Tom died in his sleep ten days ago. That was Friday, April 11.

I was Tom's wife for twenty-nine years. He was a fine husband. We had a happy life.

When Tom died, I telephoned his sister Fran right away. She and her husband Mike arrived from Texas that night. My two sons, Sam and John, came with their wives. The family helped me plan the services.

I liked the services. Tom looked very nice. Many friends were at the church. Tom's family and my family were there. I cried, and they cried with me. It was a sad time, but the services helped me.

After the services, my sons and their wives were standing with me. Friends stopped to say nice things. They said that Tom was a fine man. We cried some more.

My family and I left the church and went back to the apartment. Friends came with many things to eat. We ate and we listened to family stories. My sons heard some of the stories for the first time. We cried and we laughed at these stories.

The services were on Monday, April 14. That was a week ago. My sons and their wives left that night. Fran and Mike left two days ago. I am by myself for the first time.

Things happened very fast. One day, Tom was feeling fine. The next day, he was dead. I can still see his bright smile. I can still see the love in his eyes. Why did he have to die?

I will never stop thinking of Tom. But I must start thinking of myself. I have never lived by myself in my life. I have never had a job in my life. At 49, I must start my life again. I will dry my eyes and do my best.

This letter to you has helped me. I feel a little better. Jane, you are a dear friend.

Love,
Ellen

3. Studying in the States

buy (by)	I.D.	English (Ing glish)

Lee Chan has been in the States for two months. He is studying in Dallas, Texas.

The first week that he was there, Lee had a lot to do. He had to find a place to live. He had to buy many things. He had to sign up for classes. He had to get an I.D. card. He had to get a picture for his I.D. card.

Lee had to fill in many applications. Each application asked for his name, address, age, date of birth, place of birth, and sex. Lee got tired of filling in applications. He got tired of standing in line. But, at last, he was ready to start classes.

Lee has been going to class for five weeks. He has been studying very hard. His English is getting much better.

Lee's classes are three miles from where he lives. He had to buy a bicycle. Sometimes, he rides his bicycle to class. Sometimes, he takes the bus.

Lee misses his wife and child in China. But he is making many friends in the States. Two of his friends are Fran and Mike White. The Whites helped Lee find a place to live. They helped him find a bicycle to buy. They are helping him learn English. Lee visits the Whites every Saturday.

Lee likes his life in the States. He likes his classes. He is learning English very well. Lee thinks that prices in the States are high. But he thinks that the people are nice.

4. The Mile Race

as (az)	finish (fin ish)	that's

It was the day of the mile race. Fran White ate breakfast, but she didn't eat lunch. "If I eat lunch, I cannot run fast in the race," she said.

Fran's husband Mike went to the race with her. It was a nice day. The sky was bright, and the air was dry. Retired women from five cities were there for the race.

The race started at two o'clock. There were fifteen women in the race. They were at the starting line. When they heard the gun, they started running.

At first, Fran was far behind. She tried harder, and she ran faster. One by one, Fran passed thirteen women. One woman was still running next to Fran. "If I run faster, I can pass her," Fran was thinking. "But I'm running as fast as I can."

The finish line was in sight. Fran ran fast, but the other woman ran as fast as Fran. The two women passed the finish line. It was a tie!

"Nice work!" Mike said to his wife. "You were flying when you passed the finish line. A tie is just fine!"

Fran dried her face and smiled. "That's right!" she said. "It's better to be first, but a tie is not bad."

ō

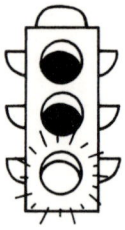

go

ō

	open	ō pen	open
	broken	brō ken	broken
	stolen	stō len	stolen
	sofa	sō fu	sofa
	old	ōld	old
	told	tōld	told

The Door Was Open

Tony (Tō ny)	oh (ō)	door (dor)	we'll (wēl)	someone (some one)
Romano (Rō mon ō)	so (sō)	both (bōth)	police (pu lēs)	anyone (any one)
		gold (gōld)	officer (of is er)	

Tony Romano lived in a big apartment building. One evening after work, Tony got back to his apartment very late. The door was open, and the lock was broken.

"Oh, no!" Tony said. "Someone has broken into my apartment. I'll go next door and telephone the police."

Tony told the police, "My name is Tony Romano. I live at 118 Valley Drive, Apartment 10-B. Someone has broken into my apartment. The door was open when I arrived from work. The door was open, and the lock was broken. I cannot tell if anyone is in there, so I didn't go in. I am telephoning from next door."

"You did the right thing," said the police officer. "We'll send a car right away."

Two police officers arrived very quickly. Both of them had guns. One officer went into Tony's apartment. The other one stayed at the door. They didn't find anyone, so both officers went next door to get Tony.

"Are you Tony Romano?" one officer asked.

"Yes, I am," Tony said. "Did you find anyone?"

"No one was there when I went in," said the other officer. "But someone has been there. Let's go and see what was stolen."

"Oh, my sofa!" said Tony. "My sofa was stolen! It was a gold sofa, and it wasn't very old." Tony looked here and there. "Both my color TV and my clock radio were stolen," he said.

Tony looked some more. "An old gold ring is missing," he told the police. "It was an old gold wedding ring. It was my mother's, so I loved it."

"Is any money missing?" asked one officer.

"Just ten dollars," Tony told her. "I never have much money in the apartment. But will I ever get my things back?"

"We'll work on it," said the police officer. "We'll see if anyone in the building can help us."

After the police left, Tony fixed his lock and went to bed. "I'm happy that my bed wasn't stolen," he said.

Story Checkup

Write Tony's story in four or five sentences.

sale

After Tony Romano's sofa was stolen, he needed another one. Tony didn't have much money, so he looked at ads in the paper. He looked for an old sofa.

These are the ads that Tony looked at. Read them, and write short answers to the questions.

FOR SALE

Green sofa with matching chair. 2 years old. $250 for both. 472-1653 after 5.

Kitchen table and four chairs, painted white. Very nice. $50. 946 Second Street. Must sell this week.

Apartment sale: sofa, coffee table, large rug, chairs, dishes, pans. 205 Valley Drive. Saturday, 9 a.m. to 4 p.m.

FOR SALE

Gold sofa—$75, green curtains—$15, bed—$40, black and white TV—$30, 2 radios—$10 each, wedding dress—$75, tent—$20. 422-9121 any time.

Old clocks, dolls, glass plates, picture frames, quart jars. Old Red Barn, 3267 River Street. Open every day from 10 a.m. to 6 p.m.

Color TV—$140, gray sofa—cost $800, will sell for $400. 476-3986.

1. Are the green sofa and chair three years old? _____

   What is the price of both? _____

   What is the telephone number? _____

2. What day is the apartment sale? _____

   Does the ad tell the price of this sofa? _____

   What is the address? _____

3. What is the price of the gold sofa? _____

4. What is the price of the gray sofa? _____

5. Which is cheaper, the gray sofa or the gold one? _____

6. Which is cheaper, the gold sofa or the green sofa and chair? _____

Practice

Read the sentence. Underline each word with the sound ō.

1. The door was open, and the lock was broken.
2. Both my clock radio and my color TV were stolen.
3. Tony's sofa was stolen.
4. An old gold ring is missing.
5. Let's go and see what was stolen.

Read the word. Write the two words that it comes from.

I'll	I	will
1. that's	_____	_____
2. we'll	_____	_____
3. didn't	_____	_____
4. I'm	_____	_____

Fill in the right word: *we'll, I'm, that's, didn't.*

1. _____ a nice sofa.
2. _____ see you at the party.
3. _____ tired of standing in line.
4. Tony _____ go into his apartment by himself.

Answer each question with a sentence.

1. Did Tony Romano live in a big apartment building or a little one?

_____

2. What was broken at Tony's apartment?

_____

3. Where did Tony go to telephone the police?

_____

4. Why did Tony love the gold ring that was stolen?

_____

Say the word. Write the number of syllables.

1. someone _____
2. police _____
3. officer _____
4. broken _____
4. sofa _____
6. telephone _____
7. arrived _____
8. quickly _____
9. sale _____
10. missing _____

o—e = ō

home = hōm

o—e = ō

	robe	robe rōb	robe
	nose	noze nōz	nose
	woke	woke wōk	woke
	smoke	smoke smōk	smoke
	phone	fone fōn	phone
	alone	u lone u lōn	alone

A Fire at Home

Rose (Roze)	Joe (Jō)	smell	department (dē part ment)
Stone	cold (cōld)	fire	cigarette (sig u ret)
hope		glad	

It was late at night. Joe Stone was home alone. He had on his robe. He was smoking in bed while he watched TV. Joe never smoked in bed while his wife, Rose, was home. But he sometimes smoked in bed when he was alone.

Joe went to sleep with his cigarette in his hand. The cigarette didn't burn Joe's robe, but it did burn the bed covers. Smoke filled the air.

Joe was sleeping, so he did not smell the smoke. But Joe's puppy smelled the smoke. The puppy jumped on the bed and put its cold nose on Joe's face. The puppy's cold nose woke Joe up.

When Joe woke up, the bed was on fire. "I must phone the fire department, but not from here," he said. "I'll go next door to phone." Joe picked up the puppy and ran into the cold night. He ran next door and phoned the fire department.

The fire department worked fast. A fire truck arrived at Joe's home very quickly. Joe was standing in the street.

Men and women came on the fire truck. "Is anyone in there?" one of them asked Joe.

"No," Joe answered. "I was home alone. I'm glad that you are here. I hope that you can save my home."

The men and women started putting water on the fire. Joe watched them with the puppy in his arms. It was cold, so Joe put the puppy in his robe.

Rose Stone came home while the fire was burning. She ran to her husband. "Oh, Joe!" she said. "I'm glad that you are OK. We worked very hard to buy this home. I hope that they can save it."

Rose picked up the puppy and patted its nose. "I'm glad that you saved the puppy," she said.

"I didn't save him," said Joe. "He saved me. He smelled the smoke and woke me up. I was smoking in bed, but I have learned my lesson."

"I hope so," said Rose.

The people from the fire department saved the Stones' home. The Stones thanked the men and women for saving their home.

Story Checkup

Read these eight sentences.
What happened first? Put a number 1 by that sentence.
Put the right numbers by the other sentences.

_____ Joe went to sleep.

_____ Joe phoned the fire department.

_____ Joe was smoking in bed.

_____ Rose Stone came home.

_____ The cigarette burned the covers.

_____ The puppy smelled the smoke.

_____ A fire truck arrived at Joe's home.

_____ The puppy woke up Joe.

don't (dōnt)	anything (any thing)	everyone (every one)

Phoning for help

Keep the numbers of the police and fire department by your telephone. If you need help, you can find the phone number quickly.

What do you say when you phone the fire department?

1. Give your name.
2. Give your street address.
   Add anything that will help them find you.
3. Tell what has happened.
4. Give the other person time to ask you more.

What Joe said on the phone

This is what Joe Stone told the fire department when he phoned. Did Joe say the right things?

Joe Stone: This is Joe Stone. There is a fire in my home. It's at 1428 Garden Drive. That's not far from Second Street. The fire started in a bed at the back of the building.

Fire department: Where are you?

Joe Stone: I'm phoning from next door.

Fire department: Is everyone away from the building?

Joe Stone: Yes, I was home alone.

Fire department: Fine. Don't go back home. Don't try to save anything.

If you have a fire

Here are some other things to think of if you have a fire.

1. Get everyone away from the burning building fast.
   Don't stop to telephone. Don't stop to take anything with you.
2. Phone the fire department from next door or from a pay phone.
3. Never go back into a burning building.

Practice

Read the sentences. Underline each word with the sound ō.

1. Joe Stone was home alone.
2. Joe was smoking in bed.
3. The puppy's cold nose woke up Joe.
4. I hope that you can save my home.
5. Joe put the puppy in his robe.
6. I will not phone from here.

Read the big word. Then write the two little words that you see in it.

anything	any	thing
1. someone	_____	_____
2. anyone	_____	_____
3. everyone	_____	_____
4. myself	_____	_____
5. himself	_____	_____
6. yourself	_____	_____

Homework

Write a short *yes* or *no* answer.

1. Was Joe home alone? _____
2. Did the cigarette burn Joe's robe? _____
3. Did Joe phone from his home? _____
4. Did the puppy save Joe's life? _____
5. Did the fire department save the Stones' home? _____

Read each word. In List 1, write the word with *-ing*.
In List 2, write the word with *-d* or *-ed*.

	List 1	List 2
smoke	smoking	smoked
1. phone		
2. save		
3. smell		
4. arrive		
5. answer		

oa = ō

boat = bōt

oa = ō

	coat	coat	coat
	road	road	road
	load	load	load
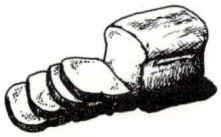	loaf	loaf	loaf
	toast	toast	toast
	roast	roast	roast

Camping in October

Joan	lake	camp	shore (shor)	over (ō ver)
rain	made	end	clothes (clōz)	October (Oc tō ber)
Oak		weekend (week end)	wear (wār)	heavy (hev y)

"Let's go camping this weekend," said Joan to her mother. "There is a state park at Green Lake. It's on Shore Road. We can rent a boat there."

"Fine," said Mrs. Oak. "I think that camping in October is fun. What shall we take to eat? Let's see, we'll need coffee, apples, cheese, eggs, and a loaf of bread. Shall we take any meat?"

"No, we'll go fishing," Joan told her mother. We can roast fish over a fire. Wear old clothes, and bring a heavy coat. It's cold at the lake in October, and sometimes it rains."

On Saturday, Joan and her mother loaded the back end of their truck. They loaded their tent and two sleeping bags into the truck. They loaded other things that they needed.

Mrs. Oak and Joan were on the road by seven o'clock. Mrs. Oak was wearing old clothes and her husband's heavy hunting coat. Joan was wearing old clothes and a heavy coat.

They got to Shore Road at eight o'clock. The state park was at the end of the road. After they put up their tent, Mrs. Oak went to rent a boat. Joan cut the loaf of bread and made cheese sandwiches.

The two women spent the day fishing on the lake. At the end of the day, they each had six fish.

When they got to the shore, Mrs. Oak made a fire and Joan cleaned the fish. Joan roasted the fish over the fire. While Joan was roasting the fish, Mrs. Oak made coffee and toast. She cut some bread from the loaf and toasted it over the fire.

After dinner, they watched the fire for a while. Then they got into their sleeping bags and went to sleep.

The next day, it rained for a while. After it stopped raining, the two women fished again. Then they went for a boat ride on the lake.

"This has been a nice weekend," said Joan. "Let's go camping again when Dad is home. Do you think that you and Dad can go next weekend?"

"Yes, I think so," said Mrs. Oak. "Your dad will like camping at this lake in October."

Story Checkup

Write short answers.

1. What month was it? _____

2. Where did Joan and her mother go camping?

_____

3. What did they take with them to eat? _____

_____

4. What other things did they take? _____

_____

5. Why did they rent a boat? _____

map way

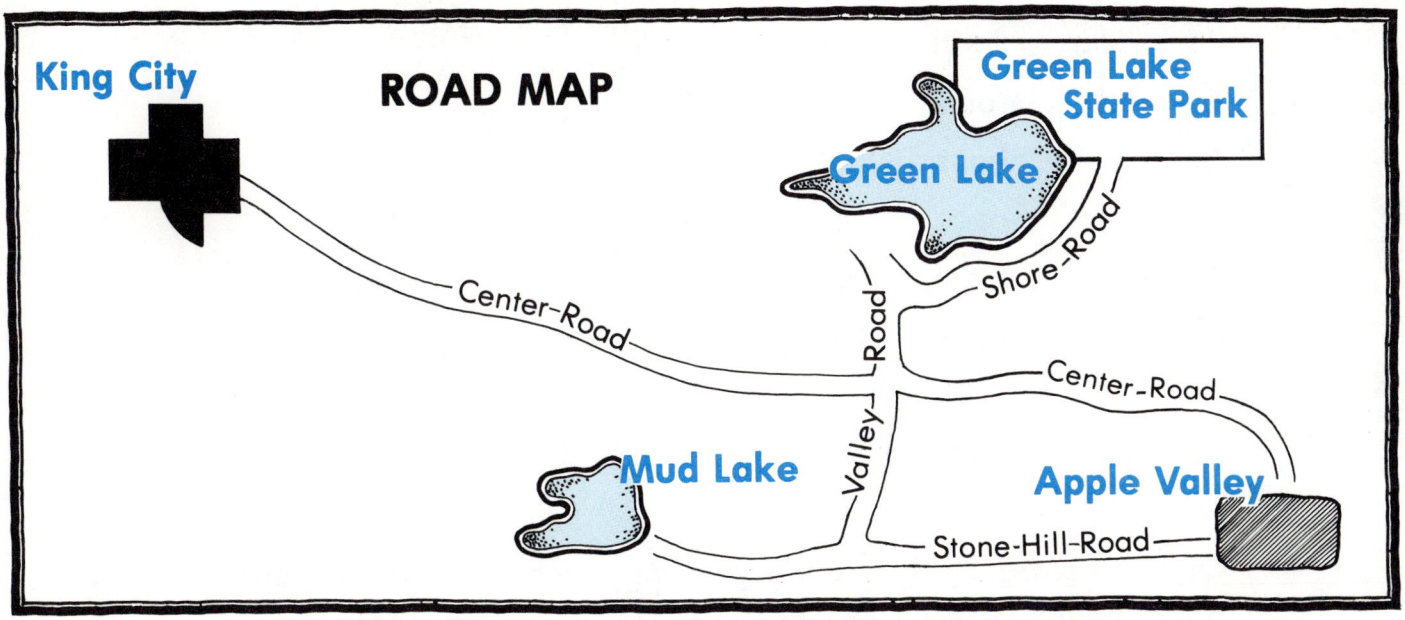

Write the answers. Find the answers by looking at the road map.

1. What road goes from King City to Apple Valley?

_____

2. What is the best road to take from Apple Valley to Mud Lake?

_____

3. The Oaks live in King City. Which roads do they take to the state park?

_____ _____

_____

Circle the right answers. Find the answers by looking at the map.

1. Mrs. Oak and Joan are on their way to the state park. They are on Center Road. When they get to Valley Road, which way do they turn? Left Right
2. They are on Valley Road. When they get to Shore Road, which way do they turn? Left Right

Practice

Say the words. Circle the words with the sound ō.

1.	Joan	John	Joe	Jason
2.	red	road	Rosa	robe
3.	bat	boat	both	box
4.	cold	cop	coat	come
5.	top	toast	roast	best
6.	left	love	load	loaf

Copy the word. Add the ending -y. Make a change in the word if you have to. Write one of the words in each sentence.

wind windy fun funny

rain _____ sun _____

sleep _____ rock _____

1. It's fun to be at the shore on a _____ day.
2. It's not fun to be there on a _____ day.
3. Carla put her _____ child to bed.
4. Joan does not like to run on the _____ path.

Homework

Answer with the name of a person in the story.

1. Who went to rent a boat? _____
2. Who made cheese sandwiches? _____
3. Who cleaned the fish? _____
4. Who roasted the fish? _____
5. Who made coffee and toast? _____

Read the big word. Then write the two little words that you see in it.

anyone	any	one
1. weekend	_____	_____
2. everyone	_____	_____
3. homework	_____	_____
4. cannot	_____	_____
5. someone	_____	_____
6. anything	_____	_____
7. yourself	_____	_____

ōw = ō

snow = snō

ōw = ō

	blow	blōw	blow
	show	shōw	show
	know	nōw	know
	throw	thrōw	throw
	window	win dōw	window
	follow	fol ōw	follow

Stuck in the Snow

slowly (slōw ly)	below (bē lōw)	wind	side	you're (your)
yellow (yel ōw)	zero (zē rō)	sand	ice (ise)	onto (on to)
				ahead (u head)

It is snowing, and the wind is blowing. It is five below zero. The wind is blowing so hard that it feels much colder. It feels like forty below zero. There is snow and ice on the road.

Sam is on his way home from hockey practice. He is driving his father's car. Sam knows that he must drive slowly in the snow. It is snowing so hard that Sam cannot see the road. He follows the lights of the car ahead of him.

The wind blows snow onto Sam's car windows. Sam stops by the side of the road. He cleans the snow and ice from his windows.

A yellow car passes Sam. It is not going slowly. The yellow car throws more ice and snow onto Sam's windows.

Sam cleans his windows again. "He is driving very fast," Sam thinks. "He is going so fast that he will miss the turn up ahead."

Sam gets back in his car and drives slowly. When he comes to the turn in the road, he sees the yellow car again. It is on the side of the road. It is stuck in the snow and ice. Sam stops to help the driver.

The man says, "I'm stuck, and I don't know what to do."

"I have a bag of sand in my car," says Sam. "I'll throw some sand under your wheels." Sam throws sand under the wheels of the car.

Then Sam tells the man to rock the car. "Drive ahead a little. Then drive back," he says. "Then drive ahead a little more. Make a path in the snow." But the man does not know what to do.

"Here, let me show you," Sam says. He gets into the man's car on the driver's side. Sam shows him what to do. Sam rocks the car and gets it onto the road again.

The man says, "You're not very old, but you know a lot. Thanks for showing me. If this ever happens again, I'll know what to do."

Sam says, "It's no fun to get stuck when it's below zero. I was glad to help you. If you're going my way, you can follow me. Follow the lights of my car."

Story Checkup

Write the story in three or four sentences.

_____

_____

_____

_____

_____

_____

_____

Read these traffic signs.

speed limit (lim it)

Practice

Copy the word. Add the ending -y to each word.
If the word ends with e, drop the e and then add -y.
Write one of the words in each sentence.

smoke _____ snow _____

ice _____ sand _____

1. We camped on the _____ shore.
2. The _____ air hurts my eyes.
3. I will not drive on _____ roads.

Copy the word. Add the ending -*ly*.
Then write one of the words in each sentence.

quick _____ glad _____

slow _____ light _____

sad _____ cheap _____

1. Sam drives _____ in the snow.
2. The boy looked at his dead puppy _____.
3. It was raining _____, but we went fishing.
4. If I work _____, I can finish by three o'clock.

Homework

Write a short *yes* or *no* answer.

1. Does Sam drive slowly in the snow? _____
2. Does Sam's car get stuck? _____
3. Is it forty below zero? _____
4. Is Sam on his way to hockey practice? _____
5. Does Sam help the man in the yellow car? _____
6. Does Sam throw sand under the car wheels? _____

Drop the ending from each word. Write the word that is left.
Make a change in the word if you have to.

having have shopped shop

1. stopped _____
2. loaded _____
3. windy _____
4. icy _____
5. smoking _____
6. rained _____
7. quickly _____
8. slowly _____
9. sleeping _____
10. running _____

Lesson 20

York

or

or

ore = or

store

ore = or

40	forty	for ty	forty
	short	short	short
	corner	cor ner	corner
	tore	tore	tore
	before	bē fore	before

At the Department Store

wore	fourth (forth)	than	what's
sport	floor (flor)	want (wont)	cheapest (cheap est)
shirt	Porter (Port er)	most (mōst)	salesperson (sales person)
sleeve		close (cloze)	

Steve was hurrying up York Street. He was on his way to Porter's Department Store. Porter's was on the corner of York Street and Fourth Street.

Steve's friend David was at the corner. "What's the hurry?" David asked.

"I have to buy a sport shirt before the store closes," Steve said. "I wore my brother's best sport shirt last night, and I tore it. I tore the sleeve on the car door."

"One time, I wore my father's shirt and tore it," David said. "He's still angry that I wore his shirt."

"I want to buy another shirt like my brother's before he gets home," said Steve. "I'm in a hurry. See you later."

Steve looked at a sign on the first floor. It said that men's clothes were on the fourth floor. Steve hurried up to the fourth floor. He went to the men's department. "I want a yellow shirt with short sleeves," he told the salesperson.

"The shirts with short sleeves are over there," said the salesperson.

Steve picked up a red shirt with short sleeves. It cost fourteen dollars. A green shirt cost twenty dollars. "That one costs more than the red one, but it's a better shirt," said the salesperson. "And this yellow one is Porter's best sport shirt," he added.

Steve was thinking, "The best shirt will cost the most." And he was right. The yellow shirt did cost the most. It cost thirty dollars.

"I have forty dollars," Steve was thinking. "The green shirt is cheaper than the yellow one, and the red shirt is the cheapest. But I will have to buy the one that costs the most. The yellow shirt is like my brother's."

"The store is going to close," the salesperson said. "Do you want to buy anything before it closes?"

"Yes," said Steve, "I'll take the thirty-dollar shirt. Here is forty dollars."

Steve got back some change from his forty dollars. He picked up the shirt and hurried to the corner. On the bus, he was thinking, "It cost me thirty dollars to wear a shirt one time! I'll never wear my brother's clothes again."

Story Checkup

order (or der)

In what order did these things happen?
Put a number by each sentence to show the right order.
If you don't know the order, please read the story again.

_____ Steve was hurrying up York Street.

_____ Steve tore his brother's shirt.

_____ Steve looked at a sign on the first floor.

_____ The salesperson showed Steve the best shirt in the store.

_____ Steve got back some change.

_____ Steve gave the salesperson forty dollars.

& (and) directory (di rec tor y)

Porter's Department Store			
FIRST FLOOR	**SECOND FLOOR**	**THIRD FLOOR**	**FOURTH FLOOR**
Garden Shop Bake Shop Clocks & Watches Coffee Shop Paper	***Women's Clothes*** Skirts, Shirts Dresses, Hats ***Children's Department*** Children's Clothes Baby Clothes	***For the Home*** Beds Sofas & Chairs Dishes Curtains Radios & TVs	***Men's Department*** Coats Shirts ***Sports Department*** Bicycles Tents Boats

This is a store directory. A store directory is a sign. It tells where to find things in the store. The directory is on the first floor. Some stores have a directory on every floor.

Look at this store directory, and answer the questions below.

1. On which floor can you find men's coats? _____
2. On which floor can you find a dress for a baby? _____
3. On which floor can you buy a radio? _____
4. On which floor can you get something to eat? _____
5. Where is the sports department? _____
6. Which floor has things for camping? _____
7. In which shop can you get a loaf of bread? _____
8. Which floor has things for the kitchen? _____

Practice

Say the words. Circle the words with the sound or.

1.	shirt	short	hurt	shore
2.	tore	wore	are	fire
3.	brother	order	corner	burn
4.	sport	start	floor	door
5.	turn	store	wear	York

Add *-er* to each word, and write the *-er* word in List 1.
Add *-est* to each word, and write the *-est* word in List 2.

	List 1	List 2
cheap	cheaper	cheapest
1. slow	_____	_____
2. fast	_____	_____
3. short	_____	_____
4. high	_____	_____
5. light	_____	_____
6. bright	_____	_____
7. clean	_____	_____

Write the missing number word.

first, third, thirty, fourth, fourteen, forty

1. Steve looked at a sign on the _____ floor.
2. He looked at sport shirts on the _____ floor.
3. The cheapest shirt cost _____ dollars.
4. The best shirt cost _____ dollars.
5. Steve gave the salesperson _____ dollars.

Write the missing endings: *-ing, -ed, -y, -ly, -er, -est.*

1. Sam drives the car very slow_____.
2. Steve looks at three shirts, but he doesn't buy the cheap_____ one.
3. Kitty lives in a wind_____ city.
4. Steve was hurry_____ up York Street.
5. Mrs. Oak toast_____ the bread over the fire.
6. I am short_____ than my brother.

More Reading with ā, ē, ī, ō, or

paper ā	cake a–e	paint ai		day ay
we ē	Pete e–e	eat ea	see ee	key ey
I ī	time i–e	tie ie	night igh	my y
go ō	home o–e	boat oa	snow ōw	
York or	store ore			

1. The Ring That Was Stolen

broke stole

One day in October, a police officer phoned Tony Romano. "This is Officer Roberts," she said. "I came to your home when someone broke into it. We think that two men stole your things. We think that we have both men."

Tony said, "Did you find my old gold ring? I hope so."

The officer told him, "Come to the police department, and we'll show you a ring. We think that it is yours."

Tony asked, "Did you find my sofa and other things?"

The officer said, "No, we don't have them yet. If we find anything, we'll let you know."

After a while, Tony got his gold ring back. But he never got back the other things that were stolen.

2. Joe Quit Smoking

quit	morning (morn ing)
won't (wōnt)	instead (in sted)

The morning after the fire, Joe Stone quit smoking. "I'm throwing my cigarettes away," he said. "I won't start another fire in my home."

His wife Rose was glad. She wanted Joe to live many more years. She didn't like smoke in her eyes and nose. She didn't like the smell of smoke in her clothes.

But it was hard for Joe to quit. "I have been smoking for forty years," he said. "If I quit, I won't have anything to do with my hands."

Every morning, Joe wanted a cigarette when he woke up. But he got up and made toast instead. He wanted to smoke when he was home alone. But he painted his boat instead. Joe wanted a cigarette every night before he went to sleep. But he kissed Rose instead.

One morning, Joe told Rose, "I have not smoked for four months. I won't ever smoke again."

3. The End of a Cold Night

forget (for get)	young (yung)	Jones (Jōnz)

When Bob Jones got stuck in the snow and ice, Sam helped him get his car onto the road again. Then Mr. Jones followed Sam's car. At the corner of Oak and Shore Roads, both cars stopped. Sam opened his window and yelled, "I'm turning here. Can you find your way alone? Your brother's home is two miles ahead. It's at the end of the road. Don't forget to drive slowly."

Mr. Jones yelled back, "I won't forget. Thanks a lot. You're a fine young man."

At his brother's home, Mr. Jones told his story. "I was stuck in the snow. The wind was blowing hard, and it was below zero. A young man stopped to help me. I will never forget that young man. He saved my life."

4. A Shirt Story

"Where is my yellow sport shirt?" Tom asked his brother.

Steve said, "I wore it last night, and I tore it on the car door."

"What?" said Tom. "You tore my best shirt! I wanted to wear it tonight."

Don't be angry," said Steve. "I got you another one at Porter's Department Store. See, it's yellow, and it has short sleeves just like yours. It cost me thirty dollars."

"Oh," said Tom. "I got my shirt on sale. It was cheaper than this one. You're not a bad brother. You can wear my sport coat if you want to."

"No, thanks," said Steve. "I'm going to a party this weekend, but I'll wear my old coat."

music

ū

	United States	ū nīt ed	United States
	Cuba	Cū bu	Cuba
	menu	men ū	menu
	university	ū ni ver si ty	university
	refugees	ref ū jeez	refugees
	future	fū cher	future

Laubach Way to Reading

Checkups for Skill Book 3

3

Name _____

Date _____

Checkup 1

Say the vowel sound. Circle each word with that sound.

ē	me	met	see	at	eaten

ā	pan	pay	cake	back	nail	baby	key
ē	key	need	Pete	pet	tea	ten	we
ī	by	time	did	die	high	hit	child
ō	got	go	cold	snow	road	rock	robe
ū	must	music	menu	Hugo	Hunt	union	uncle
or	for	from	more	short	floor	word	born

KW HARRIS COUNTY PUBLIC LIBRARY
KINGWOOD BRANCH LIBRARY

ISBN 0-88336-933-8

© 1983 by New Readers Press, Publishing Division of Laubach Literacy International,
Box 131, Syracuse, NY 13210 / All rights reserved. / Printed in the United States of America.

9 8

Checkup 2

Read the word. Write the number of syllables.

alone _____	department _____

1. before _____
2. slowly _____
3. cheese _____
4. radio _____
5. application _____
6. yesterday _____
7. university _____
8. salesperson _____

Checkup 3

Read the big word. Then write the two little words you see in it.

anything	_____	_____

1. landlady _____ _____
2. underline _____ _____
3. yourself _____ _____
4. timetable _____ _____
5. sometimes _____ _____
6. everyone _____ _____
7. weekend _____ _____
8. payday _____ _____

Checkup 4

Read the word. Write the two words that it comes from.

what's	_____	_____	don't	_____	_____

1. I'm	_____	_____	6. didn't	_____	_____
2. it's	_____	_____	7. you're	_____	_____
3. can't	_____	_____	8. we'll	_____	_____
4. won't	_____	_____	9. wasn't	_____	_____
5. I'll	_____	_____	10. let's	_____	_____

Checkup 5

Drop the ending from each word. Write the word that is left. Make a change in the word if you need to.

crying	_____	dried	_____

1. windy	_____	6. started	_____
2. tied	_____	7. brighter	_____
3. flying	_____	8. slowly	_____
4. tries	_____	9. biggest	_____
5. baker	_____	10. cities	_____

Add the ending *-s* or *-es* to each word. Make a change in the word if you need to. Write the word with the ending.

day	_____	city	_____

1. party _____
2. key _____
3. boy _____
4. family _____

Add the ending *-d* or *-ed* to each word. Make a change in the word if you need to. Write the word with the ending.

stay	_____	marry	_____

1. play _____
2. cry _____
3. die _____
4. paint _____
5. save _____
6. dry _____

Write the missing ending: *-y, -ly, -er, -est.*

Joan was the fast_____ runner in the race.

1. Lee drives the car very slow_____.
2. Steve is short_____ than his brother.
3. I do not like to drive on a snow_____ day.
4. This is the cheap_____ shirt in the store.

Checkup 6

Circle the right word.

Rosa is sitting at the	take	table	little

1. David got a glass of	milk	mark	cold
2. Carla started work in	Arthur	April	Friday
3. Kay writes a check for the	rent	spent	rain
4. Jason will paint the	stairs	story	hairs
5. The wedding cake was on a	play	late	plate
6. We spent a hundred	doors	dolls	dollars
7. This is the best salad I have ever	eat	eaten	each
8. Ms. Smith is Carla's	teach	teacher	teeth
9. Pete likes to play	hockey	happy	hurry
10. I am getting a driver's	plate	license	light
11. Lee is on a night flight from	child	China	Chan
12. The puppy smelled the	stole	smoke	nose
13. Mrs. Oak made coffee and	toast	tents	test
14. Joan wore her old	class	clothes	close
15. The man's car was stuck in the	snack	snow	show
16. Steve was on his way to the	store	story	stole
17. He looked at the sign on the first	four	floor	fly
18. The refugees came from Cuba on a	bat	boat	both
19. Rosa didn't know the words on the	union	men	menu
20. Hugo looked forward to a better	future	picture	fourth

Checkup 7

Listen to each word, and write it.

1. _____
2. _____
3. _____
4. _____
5. _____
6. _____
7. _____
8. _____
9. _____
10. _____

Listen to each sentence, and write it.

1. _____
2. _____
3. _____
4. _____
5. _____

Checkup 8

Read each story, and answer the questions after it. Write a short answer to each question.

Story 1

Carla's class had a party in the park. The men and women ran races. Jason was the fastest runner. After the races, they sat under the trees for lunch. They had potato salad, ham sandwiches, and cake to eat. They had iced tea to drink. Everyone had a fine time.

1. Who had a party? _____
2. Where was the party? _____
3. Who was the fastest runner? _____
4. What kind of sandwiches did they have to eat? _____
5. What did they have to drink? _____

Story 2

Jane and Tony are in a coffee shop for breakfast. They are looking at the menu.

"I'll just have toast and coffee," says Jane.

Tony says, "I'll have ham and eggs. And I'll have milk to drink."

1. Where are Jane and Tony? _____
2. What are they looking at? _____
3. What meal will they order? _____
4. Who will have ham and eggs? _____
5. Who will drink coffee? _____

Checkup 9

Read this ad, and answer the questions.

VALLEY MARKET

Ham $2.19

Hamburger $1.87

Large **Eggs** $1.09

Ice 89¢ a bag

Milk
Quart 55¢
Half Gallon 98¢

Fresh Baked **Bread** $1.10 a loaf

Instant Potatoes 79¢ a box

Instant Coffee $2.25 a jar

Green Beans 3 cans for $1.00

1. What two kinds of meat are in this ad? _____ and _____
2. What is the price of a quart of milk? _____
3. What does a jar of instant coffee cost? _____
4. What does a loaf of bread cost? _____
5. What do three cans of green beans cost? _____

Checkup 10

Fill in this application.

_____
Last name First name

Date of birth: _____ Sex: M ☐ F ☐
Month/Day/Year

Address: _____
Number and street

_____
City State Zip code

_____
Sign here

A Family from Cuba

Hugo (Hū gō)	Garcia (Gar sē u)	studied (stud yd)	speak
Cuban (Cū bun)	citizen (sit i zen)	forward (for werd)	wait
union (ūn yun)	Florida (Flor i du)	became (bē came)	band
			U.S.

Hugo and Rosa Garcia came from Cuba with their three sons. The Garcia family came to the United States with other Cuban refugees.

The Cuban refugees came to the United States for a better future. They looked forward to a better future for their children. They wanted to be United States citizens.

The refugees came from Cuba on a boat. They came to Florida. At first, they lived in a refugee camp.

A family in Union Park, Florida, became friends with the Garcias. They helped the Garcias find a place to live in Union Park. They helped Hugo and Rosa find jobs.

Hugo was a music teacher in Cuba. He wanted to teach in the United States. But he didn't speak English very well. So Hugo got a job in a band. The band played on weekends. In the mornings, he cut grass and cleaned buildings at a university.

Rosa got a job in a snack shop. At first, she didn't know the words on the menu. So she had to work in the kitchen.

The Garcias had to work very hard. But they looked forward to a better future.

Rosa studied the words and prices on the menu. When she learned to read the menu, she got a better job. She waited on tables at the snack shop. Rosa liked to wait on tables. She liked to speak English with the people that came in.

Hugo got into a union. In the union, he got more money than he did before. He played in a bigger band.

The Garcias' sons looked forward to going to a university. They worked part time and saved their money. Later, each of them studied at a university in Florida.

The Garcias had to wait five years before they became U.S. citizens. They became fine citizens.

Story Checkup

Write a short answer to each question.

1. Where did the Garcias live before they came to the United States? _____

2. What state did they come to in the United States?

   _____

3. What city did they live in? _____

4. Where did Rosa work? _____

5. What job did Hugo have on weekends? _____

   _____

country (cun try)	America (U mār i cu)	near
countries (cun tryz)	Mexico (Mex i cō)	north
		biggest (big est)

Map of North America

This is a map of North America. The biggest country in North America is Canada. Two other big countries in North America are the United States and Mexico. Cuba is another country in North America.

There are 50 states in the United States. But this map shows the names of just two states, Texas and Florida. The names of these two states were in some of your lessons.

Study the map, and answer these questions. Answer with *yes* or *no*.

1. Is Canada north of the United States? _____

2. Is Mexico north of the United States? _____

3. Is the United States bigger than Mexico? _____

4. Is Cuba bigger than Mexico? _____

5. Is Cuba near the state of Florida? _____

6. Is Mexico near the state of Texas? _____

Practice

Say the words. Circle the words with the sound ū.

1.	Hugo	hunt	union	hurt
2.	cut	Cuba	church	Cuban
3.	future	United	funny	under
4.	music	men	checkup	menu
5.	young	you	studied	York

Homework

Circle *yes* or *no* to answer the question.

1. Did the Cuban refugees come to Florida on a boat?	Yes	No
2. Did Hugo teach at a university in Florida?	Yes	No
3. Did Rosa learn to speak English?	Yes	No
4. Did the Garcias become citizens in three years?	Yes	No
5. Did the Garcias' sons go to a university in Florida?	Yes	No

A Baby Brings Changes

Tell your answer to each question.

1. What changes in Jason's way of life did the baby bring?
   Which change do you think upset Jason the most?
2. What changes in Gail's way of life did the baby bring?
   Which change do you think upset her the most?
3. Why did Gail want to go back to work after the baby came?
4. Why didn't Jason want Gail to work?
5. What plan did Gail and Jason agree to try?
6. What do you think of their plan?

Write a short answer to each question.

1. What was the baby's name? _____
2. Where did Jason go one Saturday? _____
3. What two things do Gail and Mary plan to share?

   _____

Is Love Enough?

Tell your answer to each question.

1. Did Maria like to be a migrant? Why or why not?
2. What did Maria tell Carlos the first time he asked her to marry him?
3. In what ways do you think that love changed Carlos and Maria?
4. Do you like the name of the story?
   What other name can you think of for the story?

Write a short answer to each question.

1. What was one crop that Maria picked? _____
2. Who was the farmer's son? _____
3. Who helped Carlos find a teacher? _____
4. Which man did Maria love? _____

Homework

Read the word. Write the two words that it comes from.

1. we're _____ _____
2. what's _____ _____
3. you're _____ _____
4. don't _____ _____
5. won't _____ _____
6. can't _____ _____

Fill in the right word: *we're, can't, won't, what's, don't, you're.*

1. "_____ the matter?" asked Jason.
2. "_____ going to be parents," said Gail.
3. "We _____ afford a baby-sitter," said Jason.
4. "I _____ be upset," said Gail to herself.
5. "_____ nice, Carlos," said Maria.
6. "Please, Maria, _____ let Ed come near you," said Carlos.

Helen Keller

Tell your answer to each question.

1. What three handicaps did Helen Keller overcome?
2. Do you think that Anne Sullivan was a good teacher? Why or why not?
3. In what ways did Helen Keller help other handicapped people?
4. Do you like this story? Why or why not?

Write a short answer to each question.

1. When was Helen Keller born? _____
2. Was she blind and deaf from birth? _____
3. What was the first word that Helen was able to understand? _____
4. What kind of writing can many blind people read? _____

Martin Luther King Jr.

Tell your answer to each question.

1. Why did Dr. King and the others start a bus boycott?
   What change did the boycott make for blacks in Montgomery?
2. Why did blacks in Birmingham have sit-ins?
3. What big changes came from civil rights protests in the 1960s?
4. What do you think of Dr. King's way of fighting for civil rights?

Write a short answer to each question.

1. Who led blacks in their fight for civil rights?

   _____

2. What prize did he win? _____
3. What was Dr. King's age when he was killed? _____

Word List

Skill Book 3: Long Vowel Sounds introduces the 426 words and 3 symbols listed below. Variants formed by adding *-s, -es, -'s, -s', -ed, -ing,* and *-er* (comparative) to previously taught words are not listed except when *y* is changed to *i* before an ending. New words are listed in their root form when they are used with these previously taught endings. Italics indicate that a word taught earlier as a sight word is reintroduced and taught phonetically in this book.

The correlated reader, *Changes,* introduces additional words. Those words are listed at the back of that book. Lessons to accompany the correlated reader use some of those words, but they are not listed in this book.

Word	Lesson	Word	Lesson	Word	Lesson	Word	Lesson
ad	8	be	7	card	3	cried	13
again	7	beans	8	care	5	cries	13
age	12	became	22	Carla	1	cry	13
ago	15	been	12	¢ (cent)	1	Cuba	22
ahead	19	beer	7	chair	4	Cuban	22
air	13	before	20	*change	13	Dallas	11
alone	17	behind	14	cheap	8	date	5
a.m.	13	below	19	cheapest	20	David	1
America	22	best	8	check	3	day	3
& (and)	20	bicycle	11	cheese	8	dear	5
angry	7	biggest	22	child	14	depart	14
*answer	2	bill	1	China	14	department	17
anyone	16	birth	11	church	5	didn't	7
anything	17	blow	19	cigarette	17	die	13
apartment	2	boat	18	cities	14	directory	20
application	11	both	16	citizen	22	$ (dollar)	1
April	2	breakfast	12	class	1	don't	17
arrive	14	bright	14	clean	9	door	16
as	15	broke	21	close (cloze)	20	dried	13
ate	5	broken	16	clothes	18	drink	1
away	3	bus	12	coat	18	drive	11
baby	2	buy	15	coffee	1	driver	11
baby-sitter	2	by	13	cold	17	dry	13
bake	5	cake	5	corner	20	each	8
baker	8	came	5	cost	1	eat	8
band	22	camp	18	countries	22	eaten	8
bank	3	Canada	10	country	22	eight	7

*Indicates words that are introduced in titles or directions.

Word	Lesson
eighteen	7
eighty	7
eleven	7
end	18
English	15
evening	9
ever	4
every	12
everyone	17
eye	11
face	7
feel	13
fifteen	7
fifty	7
find	14
fine	15
finish	15
fire	17
flight	14
floor	20
Florida	22
fly	13
follow	19
forget	21
forty	7
forward	22
fourteen	7
fourth	20
frame	5
Friday	13
future	22
Gail	4
gallon	4
Garcia	22
gate	14
gave	5
glad	17
go	1
gold	16
gray	4

Word	Lesson
Green	7
had	3
hair	4
ham	1
hamburger	1
he	7
heavy	18
here	9
high	14
*himself	14
hockey	10
home	17
hope	17
Hugo	22
hundred	3
husband	12
I	1
ice	19
icy	19
I.D.	15
if	11
I'll	1
I'm	14
instant	2
instead	21
it's	7
Jane	5
Jason	1
Joan	18
Joe	17
Jones	21
Kay	3
keep	9
key	9
know	19
labor	9
lady	2
lake	18
landlady	4
last	3

Word	Lesson
late	7
learn	15
Lee	7
license	11
life	15
light	14
like	12
limit	19
line	13
listen	1
load	18
loaf	18
Lopez	1
love	2
made	18
make	9
map	18
Mason	3
May	3
me	2
meal	8
meat	8
menu	22
Mexico	22
Mike	12
mile	12
milk	1
*missing	1
Monday	13
money	9
month	2
*more	6
morning	21
most	20
much	5
music	1
my	1
myself	15
nail	4
near	22

Word	Lesson
need	7
never	4
next	3
nice	12
night	14
nine	7
nineteen	7
ninety	7
north	22
nose	17
Oak	18
o'clock	13
October	18
officer	16
oh	16
OK	4
old	16
onto	19
open	16
*order	20
over	18
paid	4
paint	4
paper	1
part	9
party	5
pat	2
pay	3
payday	3
people	8
permit	11
Pete	9
phone	17
place	9
plate	5
play	3
player	10
please	8
p.m.	13
police	16

Word	Lesson
Porter	20
potatoes	2
*practice	2
price	12
quart	4
*question	14
quit	21
race	12
radio	2
rain	18
Ray	3
*read	1
reader	8
refugee	22
rent	3
repair	9
retired	12
ride	11
*right	5
road	18
roast	18
robe	17
Romano	16
Rosa	2
Rose	17
sad	14
salad	1
sale	16
salesperson	20
same	11
sand	19
sandwich	1
Saturday	9
save	9
*say	2
second	9
see	7
sentence	1
service	13
seventeen	7
sex	11
shall	4
shirt	20
shore	18
*short	3
show	19
side	19
sight	14
sign	12
sixteen	7
sixty	7
sky	14
sleep	7
sleeve	20
slow	19
slowly	19
smell	17
smile	12
smoke	17
snack	1
snow	19
so	16
sofa	16
someone	16
something	8
sometimes	12
*sound	2
speak	22
speed	19
spent	3
sport	20
stairs	4
state	11
Steve	9
still	5
stole	21
stolen	16
Stone	17
store	20
stories	15
*story	1
studied	22
study	1
*syllable	2
table	2
take	5
tax	9
tea	8
teach	9
teacher	8
team	10
teenager	10
teeth	7
test	11
tester	11
Texas	11
than	20
that's	15
there	5
these	9
third	9
thirteen	7
thirty	7
throw	19
tie	13
time	11
timetable	14
tired	12
toast	18
today	3
told	16
Tony	16
tore	20
tree	7
tried	13
try	13
TV	6
*underline	14
union	22
United States	22
university	22
U.S.	22
valley	9
wait	22
want	20
wasn't	7
water	2
way	18
we	1
wear	18
wedding	5
week	9
weekend	18
we'll	16
what's	20
wheel	7
where	5
while	12
White	12
why	13
wife	12
wind	19
window	19
wives	15
woke	17
won't	21
wore	20
write	1
writer	8
written	11
year	10
yellow	19
yesterday	3
yet	5
York	1
young	21
your	3
you're	19
yourself	5
zero	19
zip code	11